Ideas of the Modern World

Nationalism

Richard Tames

HODDER
Wayland

an imprint of Hodder Children's Books

Published in Great Britain in 2003 by Hodder
Wayland, a division of Hodder Children's
Books.

This book was prepared for Hodder Wayland by
Patience Coster at Book Factory.

Series design: Simon Borrough

British Library Cataloguing in Publication Data
Tames, Richard
Nationalism. - (Ideas of the modern world)
1. Nationalism - Juvenile literature
I. Title
320.5'4

ISBN 0 7502 4368 6

Printed in Hong Kong by Wing King Tong.

Hodder Children's Books
A division of Hodder Headline Limited,
338 Euston Road, London NW1 3BH

Acknowledgements
The author and publishers thank the
following for permission to reproduce
photographs:

Camera Press: page 33; Corbis: page 19;
Mary Evans Picture Library: pages 13,
24, 27, 30; Hodder Wayland Picture
Library: pages 16 (Yale University Art
Gallery), 43 (Illustrated London News),
46; Peter Newark's Pictures: page 40;
Peter Newark's American Pictures: page
18; Peter Newark's Military Pictures:
page 22; Popperfoto: pages 9, 10 (reused
on 61), 12, 15, 17, 21, 23, 25, 31, 35, 38,
39, 44; Popperfoto/Reuter: pages 47,
54-5, 58, 59; Rex: pages 7 (reused on
contents page), 51; Topham
Picturepoint: pages 4, 8, 14, 20, 26,
29, 32, 37, 41, 45, 48 (UNEP/Allen
Tannenbaum), 52, 56-7 and title page.

Cover photo shows international flags
(Lester Lefkowitz/CORBIS)

Contents

What is Nationalism?

Nationalism is the feeling that the people of a country all belong together and are different from the peoples of other countries. The word nationalism comes from the word 'nation'. The words 'nation' and 'state' are often used to mean the same as 'country'. Historians and sociologists try to use these words more precisely.

Nations and states

A nation is a group of people whose members believe that the culture they share – expressed through language, religion, history, customs or lifestyle – binds them together in a way that makes them different and distinct from other peoples. A state is a **territory** controlled by a government.

Nationalists believe that the peoples of the world are made up of distinct nations, each of which ought to have its own state. They think that ideally all states should be **nation states**, each consisting of a single people. But for most of history this has not been the case. The most powerful states have been empires or kingdoms, often made up of different peoples.

A nation reborn – again. Demonstrators in Vilnius, the capital of Lithuania, demanding national independence in 1990. An empire five centuries ago, Lithuania was annexed by Russia in 1795, regained its independence in 1918, and was taken over again by the USSR in 1940. It finally became free once more in 1991.

Their loyalty to the government has been based on obedience to the ruler, not on the idea that people have rights and duties towards each other. Smaller states have often been based on a single city.

For example, for a thousand years Italy was divided into dozens of separate states. Italians thought of themselves not as Italians but as belonging to a city, such as Venice or Florence, or a region, like Tuscany or Sicily. The emergence of nationalism from the time of the French Revolution in 1789 (see page 19) persuaded Italians that, because they shared a common language and culture, they should unite together into a nation state.

Defining nations

In 1861 the British philosopher John Stuart Mill (1806-73) stated in his book *Representative Government*:

'A portion of mankind may be said to constitute [make up] a nationality if they are united among themselves by common sympathies which do not exist between them and any others – which make them co-operate more willingly than with other people, desire to be under the same government and desire that it should be government by themselves... '

What nationalists believe

Nationalism is based on the following set of beliefs:

1. The human race naturally consists of nations.
2. Nations can be known by features that their members share, such as race, language or religion.
3. The only rightful form of government is **self-determination** – the government of a nation by its own people. Each nation should have its own independent state and the world should be made up of nation states.

However, these beliefs are not as obviously true as nationalists have often thought. If the human race naturally consisted of nations, why had this not been clear to people before? Religions traditionally taught that being a Christian or a Muslim or a Hindu or a Jew was far more important than the country a person happened to be born in or the particular language that they spoke.

Nationalists could not agree among themselves what the signs of **nationhood** were. Some thought a nation was defined by a single language spoken by all its members and no one else, like Polish or Finnish. Others thought it was possible for a nation to speak a language shared with others – like English, Arabic or Spanish – and still be a separate nation by having a separate history or religion.

Unifying an existing nation into a single state is one way of creating a nation state, as in the case of Italy or Germany in the nineteenth century. Another way is for an existing state to take on the character of a nation, as in the case of Japan (see page 31). Another is for a nation to break away from an existing **multinational state**, like Greece (see page 22) or to throw off **colonial rule**, as in the case of Britain's thirteen **colonies** in North America (see page 16).

Throughout the nineteenth and twentieth centuries new nation states came into being. After the First World War (1914-18), the League of Nations was set up to try to solve disputes between nations peacefully. It eventually had 63 states as members. The United Nations, set up as a successor to the League after the Second World War (1939-45) now has three times as many members, because many former colonies of European states have become independent and some multinational states, like the former USSR and Yugoslavia, have split up.

Ideas and emotions

Nationalism is not just a set of ideas that appeal to people's reason. It is a powerful force which taps into people's feelings of pride, fear and hatred. Nationalism is expressed through symbols such as flags, songs, poems, legends and statues. It is an ever changing set of ideas rather than a single, fixed one. Intellectuals – for example, poets, composers and

**Newest nation – East Timor, once
a Portuguese colony, gained its
independence in 2002.**

historians – have played an important role in shaping nationalist thinking and movements.

Nations usually define themselves by a highly selective – often an imagined – view of the past. In 1882 the French historian, Ernest Renan, claimed: 'getting its history wrong is part of being a nation.' Heroes and heroic episodes are remembered, praised and magnified in importance, while shameful episodes are quietly forgotten. Renan stated that national identity depended on the sense of a shared past: 'to have performed great deeds together, to wish to perform still more – these are the essential conditions for being a people.'

New nations

The following nations have gained – or regained – their independence as states since 1990:

1990 Namibia, Yemen
1991 Armenia, Azerbaijan, Belarus, Croatia, Estonia, Georgia, Kazakhstan, Kyrgyzstan, Latvia, Lithuania, Macedonia, Moldova, Slovenia, Tajikistan, Turkmenistan, Ukraine, Uzbekistan
1992 Bosnia and Herzegovina
1993 Slovakia, Eritrea
1994 Palau
2002 East Timor

Belonging to a nation (nationhood) means that the members of that nation think of themselves as tied both to the dead of the past and the unborn of the future. Some nationalists have believed that what links these generations is their actual blood – in other words, that the Greeks or the Spanish, for example, are a distinct race. But the movement of people throughout history means that modern Greeks have little or no genetic connection with the Greeks of ancient Athens and Sparta. And the Spanish people, almost all Catholics, carry the blood of Muslim Arabs, who ruled Spain for seven centuries.

Two types of nationalism

'Ethnic nationalism' can be contrasted with 'civic nationalism'. Ethnic nationalism is based on belief in inheritance. It is genetic and historical. It is 'closed', because only those sharing the bonds of blood and belonging can be fellow nationals. Civic nationalism is based on the commitment to certain shared values. Civic nationalism is 'open', in the sense that anyone can become a national by accepting the duties of a **citizen**.

Civic nationalism ignores claims of blood or race. It is most clearly seen in nations that are made up mainly of immigrants from other countries, such as the United States, Canada, Australia or Argentina. Newcomers, after living there for a period, make a pledge of allegiance to their new country and swear

New nations built by immigrants, like the USA, offer citizens the chance to forge new identities.

On being American

As President Theodore Roosevelt declared in 1909:

'Americanism is a question of principle, of purpose, of idealism, of character. It is not a matter of birthplace or creed or line of descent.'

to obey its laws and thereby become citizens, regardless of their birth or former nationality. About half of all nations permit **dual citizenship** where a person is a citizen of two states.

The Danes are a small but ancient nation, who in the past have ruled Norway, Sweden and England as well as their own homeland. The Danish flag, flown since the thirteenth century, is the world's oldest national flag. Above, the Danes turn out in force to cheer their queen.

Patriotism or nationalism?

'Patriotism is when love of your own people comes first; nationalism is when hate for people other than your own comes first.'

Charles De Gaulle (1890-1970), war hero and president of France.

'By "patriotism" I mean devotion to a particular place and a particular way of life, which one believes to be the best in the world but has no wish to force on other people.... Nationalism, on the other hand, is inseparable from the desire for power. The abiding purpose of every nationalist is to secure more power and more prestige, not for himself but for the nation.'

George Orwell, British writer, 1945.

Scotland

The history of Scotland shows how a nation grew out of conflicting groups of peoples, became a state, then became part of another state and may become a separate and independent state yet again. It also shows how a sense of national identity and nationalism is created through conflict, culture, institutions, heroes, poets and the symbols of nationhood.

The Picts originally lived in Scotland. The Scots who, like the Picts, spoke a **Celtic** language, invaded south-west Scotland from their home in Ireland in around CE 500. The Picts and Scots fought, then blended with later arrivals – Vikings from Scandinavia and Anglo-Normans from England. In CE 843, Scotland was united under one king, although fighting between rival lords and tribal chiefs continued. But when the English king, Edward I (1272-1307), tried to conquer Scotland, the Scots united against him. In 1320, leading Scots signed the Declaration of Arbroath, swearing that as long as there were a hundred of them left alive they would never surrender to English rule. Scots claimed St Andrew as their **patron saint** and adopted his blue-and-white flag as their national banner.

England finally recognized Scottish independence in 1328. However, border wars and raiding continued until 1603, when James VI of Scotland became James I of England (after the death of

Scots in national dress gather to mark the 700th anniversary of Scotland's victory over the English at Stirling Bridge in 1297. Note the cross of St Andrew flag and, in the background, the red lion flag of the royal house of Stuart.

Scotland – a timeline

CE 843	Scotland united under a single king, Kenneth McAlpin
1320	Scottish leaders sign the Declaration of Arbroath
1328	England recognizes Scottish independence
1603–1707	Scotland and England united under one ruler
1707	The Act of Union abolishes the Scottish Parliament
1928	Founding of the National Party of Scotland
1934	National Party of Scotland is renamed the Scottish National Party (SNP)
1979	Scots vote against devolution
1997	Scots vote in favour of devolution
1999	A separate Scottish Parliament is restored

the childless Elizabeth I). From 1603 to 1707, Scotland shared a king with England but kept its own parliament. Scots settled in Ulster (Northern Ireland) and in the American colonies. But after a disastrous attempt to found a colony in Panama brought Scotland to near bankruptcy, the country entered into a merger with England.

By the Act of Union of 1707, Scotland abolished its parliament and sent representatives to Westminster instead. But Scotland kept its own separate laws, church and education system. Robert Burns' poems and Sir Walter Scott's novels kept a distinctive Scottish culture alive. Although Scotland kept its identity, the Scots were fully part of Great Britain. Britain's first Labour Member of Parliament (MP) and first Labour prime minister were both Scots. Scots made up only 5 per cent of the population but made up 10 per cent of the army.

A nation once again?

In 1928 a National Party of Scotland was founded to campaign for full Scottish independence. But, half a century later, Scottish voters rejected even limited **devolution**, although rivalry with England in sport, especially soccer, remained strong. In 1997 Scots finally voted in favour of devolution. A separate Scottish Parliament, with limited powers, has been restored – though Scots continue to send MPs to Westminster as well. The Scottish National Party still wants complete independence, preferably by 2007, three centuries after the Act of Union.

The Birth of Modern Nationalism

Elements of nationalism can be traced back centuries, before its full emergence with the French Revolution of 1789 (see page 19). The Jews of ancient Israel thought of themselves as God's chosen people. Despite being scattered from their homeland for two thousand years, they held on to their identity through religious rituals, the use of the Hebrew language in worship and study, and the memory of their remarkable history. In 1948, a new state of Israel was re-established as a Jewish homeland.

Each year Chassidic Jews enact sacred rituals recalling the great events of Jewish history. This practice has enabled the Jews to retain their identity despite being scattered from their homeland.

Nations invent themselves

' ...take the Estonians. At the beginning of the nineteenth century they didn't even have a name for themselves.... They were just a category. Since then they've been brilliantly successful at creating a vibrant culture... the Ethnographic Museum in Tartu has one object for every ten Estonians and there are only a million of them.'

Ernest Gellner, British philosopher, 1995.

The inhabitants of the 300 **city-states** that made up ancient Greece took pride in a common culture based on religion, the Greek language and a passion for athletics and argument. But the Greeks were too divided by local loyalties to become one nation. The only time they united was against a common enemy – Persia. Finally they were conquered by outsiders, the Macedonians, and then the Romans in 146 BCE.

Developing a national identity

Ancient Rome was a multi-ethnic empire based not on nationality, but on citizenship. Originally only Roman men were **citizens**, with the right to take part in politics. Then citizen rights were given to other Italians and later to non-Italians after army service. Finally all adult men under Roman rule were given citizenship, regardless of birth or language, though women and slaves – the majority of the population – were not. In CE 212, citizenship was granted to all free-born people.

An emperor and his son parade through Ancient Rome, surrounded by enthusiastic crowds.

For a thousand years after the break-up of the Roman Empire, the strongest political loyalties were local – to a king, lord or city. Europeans, however, shared a common Christian culture, Catholic in the west, **Orthodox** in the east. From the sixteenth century onwards, the more successful European kingdoms such as England, Spain and France created powerful central governments that imposed greater uniformity in law, religion and language, etc.

The emergence of Protestantism from 1517 onwards destroyed the common Catholic culture of Western Europe and gave wars between states the added dimension of religious hatred. Some countries, like Italy and Spain, remained Catholic, while others, such as England and Sweden, became Protestant. At the same time Latin stopped being the common

The Spanish Inquisition burning heretics in 1739. Captured British seamen, being Protestants, feared they might suffer the same fate.

European language of government and religion and was replaced by English, French, Spanish and so on. This limited the communication *between* different nations while increasing communication *within* them. During the seventeenth and eighteenth centuries, wars over **territory** and trade further sharpened the sense of identity of the ruled as English, French or Spanish etc.

The Romantic Movement

The American Revolution in 1776 (see page 16) and the French Revolution in 1789 (see page 19) happened at the same time as the Romantic Movement in Europe. The Romantic Movement rejected what the intellectuals of the previous century had valued – order, harmony, moderation – in favour of passion, adventure and struggle. Scholars and writers led the way in rediscovering national 'roots' in folklore, legend and language.

The search for national identity was especially intense in Germany, a nation split up into dozens of small kingdoms and city-states. These nevertheless shared a common language and culture. The brothers Grimm, now remembered for fairy tales, were also serious students of the German language, and began writing its dictionary. Johann Herder (1744-1803) collected folksongs, wrote about German art and preached that it was in the common people (the 'Volk') of Germany that the true spirit of the nation ('*Volksgeist*') was to be found. At the University of Berlin in 1807-8, Johann Fichte (1762-1814) gave a series of lectures in which he argued that German was the language from which all other languages developed. He claimed that Germans were the world's finest people.

The German philosopher and nationalist Johann Fichte.

America – a nation by stages

From 1607 onwards, British migrants settled in North America, creating thirteen separate **colonies**. Each had power over local affairs but the big questions of war, taxes and trade were decided by the British Parliament in London. From 1763 onwards, some colonial leaders began to argue that British rule was unjust and that the colonies ought to rule themselves.

American rebels actually lost the battle of Bunker Hill in 1775, but proved they could inflict severe losses on British professional soldiers. This painting, by American artist John Trumbull, was done in London more than ten years after the event.

Armed rebellion began in 1775. At first the rebels were in a minority. At least as many other Americans wanted to remain under British rule. The rest were either undecided or uninterested. As they got caught up in the fighting, however, they came to see British soldiers as foreign oppressors and increasingly supported the rebels. France, Britain's traditional enemy, sent soldiers and a navy to support the rebels. The British government finally gave up in 1783 and accepted the independence of the American colonies.

This did not, however, mean that the former colonists all suddenly thought of themselves as members of a new nation called America. When the leaders of the former colonies – now states – met to draw up a **constitution**, they jealously guarded their powers. The national government was given control of matters such as defence, but states kept control of their own criminal laws and right to raise taxes. As late as 1849, Senator and former Vice-President John C. Calhoun could state that: 'We are not a Nation, but a Union... of equal and sovereign States.'

Gradually, over the course of the century after 1783, a strong sense of American national identity

emerged. New immigration to America from many different countries meant that it was made up of people from a wide range of backgrounds. As Senator Carl Schurz argued in 1859: 'American nationality... did not spring from one family, one tribe, one country, but incorporates the vigorous elements of all civilized nations on Earth.'

Through schoolbooks and popular celebrations, American nationalism focused on the heroic figures of George Washington, commander of the rebel army and first president of the independent United States, and on the **Founding Fathers**, who drew up the US Constitution. This nationalism was expressed in the 'Stars and Bars' of the US flag and in the Fourth of July **Independence Day** celebrations.

Fireworks, seen here in New York in 2002, are a traditional part of the Fourth of July celebrations which commemorate the Declaration of Independence.

Settlers in covered wagons migrating westwards across America during the 1800s.

American nationalism was strengthened by Noah Webster's dictionary, which honoured American English as fully equal to the British original. American settlers were called upon to go westwards and claim for themselves a country the size of a continent. President John Quincy Adams (1767-1848) declared that America should be 'destined by God and nature to be the most populous and powerful people...' But even after three-quarters of a century of independence, the American sense of shared identity and loyalty to national institutions was not strong enough to prevent a civil war (1861-5), which cost 600,000 lives and was the bloodiest conflict in American history.

It was not until 1863 that **Thanksgiving Day** became a national holiday and not until after the Civil War that the phrase United States began to be used in the singular rather

The Pledge of Allegiance

The Pledge of Allegiance sworn by pupils in American schools was first written in 1892 by Boston Baptist minister Francis Bellamy to mark the 400th anniversary of Christopher Columbus' arrival in the Caribbean. Its original wording was: 'I pledge allegiance to my Flag and the Republic for which it stands, one nation, indivisible, with liberty and justice for all.' Bellamy wanted to include the word 'equality' but left it out because many school superintendents were against equality for women and non-whites. In 1954 the words 'under God' were added. This wording is now being challenged by **atheists** as unconstitutional.

than the plural ('*the* United States', instead of '*these* United States'). And it was not until 1931 that 'The Star-Spangled Banner' became the official national anthem of the USA.

The French Revolution

Modern nationalism emerged during the French Revolution (1789-1815). French support for the American struggle for independence bankrupted France, leading to a crisis in 1789. Critics of the monarchy argued that political power should flow upwards from the people to a government they elected, not downwards from a king who claimed to have been chosen by God. The French were no longer to be defined by their loyalty to a king, but by their loyalty to France.

This belief is known as popular **sovereignty** – the idea that only the people of a nation have the right to grant power to a government. In 1789 revolutionaries seized control in France. They executed the king and abolished the monarchy, replacing it with a **republic** in which rulers were elected. They got rid of the old royal flag and adopted a new one. Coins no longer had the king's head on them but symbols of the republic. Priests and aristocrats lost the right not to pay taxes. All citizens were to be equal before the law. The anniversary of the outbreak of the revolution, 14 July, became a national holiday.

French Declaration of the Rights of Man and the Citizen (1789)

'1. Men are born and remain free and equal in rights.
2. The aim of every political association is the preservation of the natural... rights of man. These rights are Liberty, Property, Safety and Resistance to Oppression.
3. The source of all sovereignty lies essentially in the Nation [that is to say, rightful power comes from the will of the people not the king].'

The Declaration also proclaimed the right of all citizens to equal treatment before the law, to take part in politics and to have freedom of religion and speech.

Until its replacement by the Euro in 2002, French coinage carried the words: Liberty, Equality, Fraternity.

Chain reaction in Europe

The French Revolution started a chain reaction of nationalist movements. When armies of French **royalist** exiles and foreign troops invaded France to crush the revolution leaders, the republic declared that every citizen was duty bound to defend it with his life. As the words of a new French national anthem proclaimed:

'Let us go, children of the fatherland,
Our day of glory has arrived.
Against us is tyranny,
The bloody flag is raised; the bloody flag is raised.
Assemble in the countryside
To cut down these savage soldiers
They come right into our arms
To cut the throats of your sons, your comrades.
To arms, citizens!
Form your battalions,
Let us march, let us march!
That their impure blood
Should water our fields.'

Napoleon's troops crossing the Danube in 1809. Twenty years earlier the Anglo-Irish thinker Edmund Burke had predicted that, although the French Revolution had begun by proclaiming liberty for all, it would end by creating a military dictatorship. And it did.

Napoleon flees after his final defeat at Waterloo. His vision of a united Europe cost over a million lives.

The French successfully pushed back this attack and began to invade neighbouring countries to spread republicanism throughout Europe. In most cases republicanism was rejected because it was imposed by force and was foreign to national traditions. After the fall of the French Emperor Napoleon in 1815, monarchies were restored and political rights limited to a minority in most countries.

In Germany, however, there was a growing pride in the part Germans had played in defeating Napoleon. Student clubs (*Burschenschaften*) were formed to practise fencing and gymnastics and sing nationalistic songs, such as 'What is the German's Fatherland?' (see box).

A nationalist anthem

'What is the German's fatherland?
Is it Prussia or the Swabian's land?
Is it where the grape glows on the Rhine?
Where sea-gulls skim the Baltic's brine?
Oh no! more grand
Must be the German's fatherland!

What is the German's fatherland?
Now name at last that mighty land!
Where'er resounds the German tongue,
Where'er its hymns to God are sung!
That is the land,
Brave German, that thy fatherland!'

'What is the German's Fatherland?', written by E. M. Arndt, a history professor, in 1812.

Nations and Empires

In the early nineteenth century, nationalism and optimism seemed to go together. **Idealistic** people in nations that had achieved their independence were often willing to fight to help others gain theirs. Sometimes governments, too, got involved. Some nations achieved independence through their own efforts, some because it suited another state that they should gain it, and some through a combination of the two. This is illustrated in the three examples below.

Greece

Between 1821 and 1833, Greece fought for independence from Ottoman Turkish rule. The Greek struggle was led by a Russian general. It was supported by Romanians and Serbs, also in revolt against the **Ottoman Empire**, and the English poet Lord Byron and a band of British and American volunteers known as the Philhellenes ('Lovers of Greece'). When it looked as though the Turks might reconquer Greece, the British, French and Russian governments united to sink an Ottoman fleet. They forced the Ottoman ruler to accept Greek independence and grant limited self–rule to the Serbs. The Greeks invited a German prince to become their first king because no Greek was acceptable to all of them.

Fighting to overthrow the rule of their Muslim Ottoman rulers, the Greeks chose Easter Day, the most important date in the Christian calendar, to raise their flag of revolt.

Belgium

Until 1795 Belgium was ruled by Austria. Then it was conquered by France. In 1815 it was handed over to Holland. In 1830 the Belgians rose against Dutch rule. When the Dutch tried to invade, Britain led other states in pressing them to accept Belgian independence, which they finally did in 1839. The British government's main motive was to ensure that a **territory** from which Britain could easily be invaded became a relatively powerless but independent state.

Poland

Between 1772 and 1795 Poland, once a mighty kingdom stretching from the Baltic to the Black Sea, was carved up between Russia, Austria and Prussia. After 1815 most Poles were under Russian rule. In 1830 they rose in revolt. No one came to their aid and the revolt was crushed, as was another in 1863. The strength of the Catholic Church and the Polish language, however, kept alive a strong sense of Polish national identity. This persisted against the influence of the Russian language and the Russian **Orthodox** Church, until the collapse of the Russian Empire allowed Poland to become independent once more in 1918.

Pope John Paul II visiting his native Poland in 2002. The Pope's own pride in his nation sustained its sense of identity during its years under Soviet communist control (1947-92).

Unification

In 1848, revolutions against **autocratic** government broke out in many parts of Western and Central Europe. An attempt to set up a parliament for a united Germany failed. So did a shortlived Hungarian **republic**. A congress in Prague demanded **autonomy** (self-government) for the Czechs under Austrian rule, but to no effect. The gaining of national independence by popular uprisings gave way to its achievement by war and diplomacy, or 'blood and iron'. This is illustrated in the following examples of the national unification of Italy and Germany.

Italy

The unification of Italy became known as the Risorgimento (rebirth or resurrection). Its strongest supporters were the urban middle class and particularly their student sons. Once again, help from outside was crucial. In 1815, north-western Italy was dominated by the kingdom of Sardinia, which included mainland Piedmont. The north-east (Lombardy and Venice) was occupied by Austria, and the south by the Kingdom of the Two Sicilies. The centre was split between the **Papal States** (states controlled by the Vatican) and the small states of Parma, Modena and Tuscany, which were effectively under Austrian control. Although **republicans** briefly seized power in the cities of Rome, Turin, Florence and Venice in 1848, their regimes all collapsed.

Count Cavour, prime minister of Piedmont, skilfully gained the support of the French emperor, Napoleon III,

Marching to destiny – Garibaldi leads the Thousand into Palermo in Sicily in June 1860. The city's people rose in their support, convincing Count Cavour to lend secret aid.

by offering him Nice and Savoy in return for military aid against Austria. Austria was defeated in 1859 and left its Italian territories, except for Venice. Shortly afterwards, Giuseppe Garibaldi and a volunteer army invaded the Kingdom of the Two Sicilies and offered its land to the king of Piedmont. Following **plebiscites** (votes) approving his position, Victor Emmanuel II became the first king of a united Italy in 1861. In 1866, Italy supported Germany in a war against Austria and received Venice as its reward.

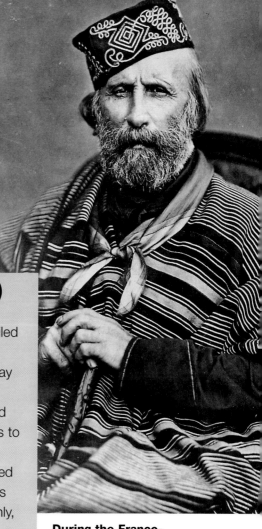

Giuseppe Garibaldi (1807-82)

Garibaldi was a sailor's son and member of a revolutionary movement, Young Italy, which failed to seize power in Genoa in 1834. He fled to South America and fought on behalf of Uruguay against an Argentine invasion. In 1848-9 he fought for the shortlived republics in Rome and Venice. In 1859 he raised a band of volunteers to fight the Austrians. 'I offer neither pay... nor provisions,' he said. 'I offer hunger, thirst, forced marches, battles and death. Let him who loves his country in his heart and not with his lips only, follow me.'

Garibaldi's exploits made him a hero on both sides of the Atlantic. In 1860 he called for more volunteers – the Thousand – to help him conquer southern Italy for Piedmont. Many British and other non-Italians felt honoured to serve under him. Garibaldi brilliantly defeated the much larger armies sent against him and then retired to live as a farmer, taking no reward or title for himself.

During the Franco-Prussian war of 1870-71 Garibaldi came out of retirement to lead a volunteer force in defence of the new French Republic.

Germany

Early nineteenth-century Germany consisted of 39 separate kingdoms, **principalities** and **city-states**, joined together in a loose **confederation**. Of these the largest was Prussia, a monarchy with a strong military tradition. The Austrian Empire was its main rival for influence over the rest. Ruled by a German-speaking minority, the Austrian Empire was a patchwork of a dozen different nationalities.

The German peoples shared a common language and were drawn together by a union to boost trade between different states. This union purposely excluded Austria. The growth of railways, the telegraph, postal services and newspapers also helped break down barriers between Germans.

The German nation was unified by Prussia, under the guidance of its chief minister, Otto von Bismarck (1815-98). In 1864 Prussia fought Denmark to **annex** the **duchies** of Schleswig and Holstein. In 1866 Prussia proposed reforming the original confederation to exclude Austria. When Austria

In 1864, German troops are welcomed by the German-speaking inhabitants of the formerly Danish-ruled duchies of Schleswig and Holstein.

The important part played by warfare in uniting Germany gave the armed forces a permanently powerful influence in the politics of the new nation.

A movement of the young

University students played a leading part in spreading nationalist ideas in Germany, Austria, Italy and France in the period after 1815. As students they were interested in ideas. Being young, without work or family ties, they had time for politics. Some were attracted by the excitement of joining secret societies. A German student, Heinrich von Gagern, wrote to his father to explain the new mood in his university: 'For the average student of the past, the university years were a time to enjoy life... their university duty was only to avoid failing the examination.... But... another group... has managed to get the upper hand.... Their purpose is to make a better future for the Fatherland... we want Germany to be considered one land and the German people one people.... Regional clubs are forbidden and we live as a German brotherhood.'

opposed this, Prussia defeated it in six weeks. Twenty-one German states north of the river Main agreed to join a North German Confederation, led by Prussia, with its capital in Berlin, the Prussian capital.

In 1870 Bismarck managed to provoke France into declaring war on Prussia. The south-German states as well as the northern ones were bound by military agreements to support Prussia. In 1871 Prussian victory over France led to all the German states forming a German Empire. The Prussian king became its emperor with the title of Kaiser (Caesar).

Empire building

In the second half of the nineteenth century the growth of **mass education**, mass-circulation newspapers and compulsory **military service** made it possible to spread the idea of 'national cultures'. The idea of **nationhood** and nationalism was glorified in art, music and literature and especially in the writing of history.

The biologist Charles Darwin (1809-82) explained the evolution of living things as a process called 'natural selection', in which the less fit species were eliminated in a struggle for survival. His theory was taken by extreme nationalists like the German general, Friedrich von Bernhardi, and applied to politics. 'War is a biological necessity,' Bernhardi wrote, 'without it an unhealthy development will follow, which excludes every advancement of the race and therefore all real civilization.'

Darwinian theories fuelled nationalism and were used to justify the building up of overseas empires in Asia, Africa and the Pacific. If, it was argued, nature itself was based on 'the survival of the fittest', then it must also be true that the stronger nations had a right to rule over weaker ones. The German historian, Heinrich von Treitschke (1834-96) declared that 'all great nations in the fullness of their strength have desired to set their mark upon barbarian lands and those who fail to take part in this great rivalry will play a pitiable role in time to come.'

The 'Scramble for Africa'

Europeans had traded with the peoples of the coast of Africa for four centuries. However, until the 1860s their knowledge of the interior of the continent was limited by disease, warlike tribes and the difficulties of transportation. These problems were solved by the introduction of the drug **quinine**, the machine gun

Seat of power? British officials lay down the law to local chiefs in East Africa in the days of colonial rule.

and the steamboat. In 1879, Leopold II of Belgium claimed the Congo, a huge portion of central Africa. In 1881, France declared that it was taking control of Tunisia. In 1882, British forces occupied Egypt. In 1884, Germany claimed Namibia, Cameroon, Togo and Zanzibar.

To avoid the possibility of war arising out of conflicting claims, the European powers came together at conferences in Berlin (1884) and Brussels (1890). Here they created frontiers for the various European **colonies**. Some of these were just chance lines across the map of the continent. Such frontiers often sliced through the territories of African peoples, so that some of them were ruled by one colonial power and others by another, with different laws and languages. Surprisingly, these frontiers have almost all lasted to the present, with none of the **post-colonial** states willing to challenge them.

Anti-imperialism

Nationalism not only fuelled **imperialism** but **anti-imperialism** too. Britain's empire was the largest. Movements for national independence challenged British rule through both peaceful and terrorist means.

Britain colonized India from 1757 onwards. Before British rule, the Indian subcontinent had been a patchwork of hundreds of princely states, loosely supervised by the **Mughal** emperor but divided by race, religion and language. The British introduced railways, schools and newspapers, and such changes united India as never before. By introducing the English language, the British provided Indian leaders with a way of communicating with each other. In 1885 the Indian National Congress was founded to press the British to share power with Indians. Later it would head the mainly peaceful movement for all-out independence (see page 42). Interestingly, some of the founders of the Congress were themselves British.

A challenge to British rule, often through terrorist means, emerged in Ireland (see page 37). A constant stream of emigrants to the USA sent back funds and volunteers to support the Fenians, an anti-British terrorist group, which organized bombings and assassinations. Many of the Irish also rejected British rule in a cultural sense, by refusing to play British sports. In 1884 the Gaelic Athletic Association was founded to promote Irish sports such as hurling and handball. Irish intellectuals such as W. B. Yeats began to revive interest in ancient myths and the Gaelic language and to put on plays with Irish themes.

British aristocrats in India hunting tigers with the local rulers. In Asia and Africa, Britain often supported native rulers. These rulers collaborated with the British in order to make their control acceptable to the ruled. Nationalist opponents of British power often therefore aimed to overthrow traditional local rulers as well as the British.

Below: a hurling final in Galway, Ireland. Irishmen who had served in the British armed forces or police were traditionally banned from taking part in nationalist sports such as hurling.

How Japan discovered it was a nation

Europeans first reached Japan in 1543, bringing Christianity with them. Japan was torn by civil war and unable to resist the newcomers or their faith. But eventually a military **dictatorship** restored order. It banned Christianity and from 1639 ended contact with the outside world for fear of foreign interference.

In 1853 a US fleet forced Japan, under threat of bombardment, to open its ports to trade. Japan's leaders knew the great Chinese Empire had been humiliated by the modern armed forces of Britain and France. To avoid the same fate, Japan began a rapid programme of modernization, using imported Western experts and technology. The ancient provinces that had been ruled by warlords were abolished and power was concentrated in the hands of a strong central government. A Western-style calendar, coinage and postal service were introduced. Compulsory education and **conscription** taught the young generation of Japanese to be loyal and obedient to their emperor. Japan gained the overseas colonies of Taiwan and Korea as a result of swift, successful wars against China and Russia. In 1902, Japan signed a treaty of alliance with Britain. In half a century, Japan had transformed itself from a backward, isolated country into one of the world's great nations.

New Zealanders of all ethnic backgrounds have come to take pride in the cultural heritage of the Maori peoples. Above, Maori men do a 'haka', the traditional challenge to combat.

Peaceful nationalism

Not all forms of nationalism were aggressive. British colonies, such as those of Canada, Australia and New Zealand developed their own distinct national identities through the peaceful development of their resource-rich lands. There was writing in English about local themes, such as **pioneering**. People in these colonies championed their own sporting heroes and adapted British customs to a different environment. But all three countries failed to bring their **native peoples** into their new sense of identity.

The histories and languages of the countries of Scandinavia were closely interlinked for a thousand years but became more distinct from one another in response to nationalist ideas. Until 1814 Norway was ruled by Denmark, but then it was handed over to Sweden. Although Norway kept its own separate government and parliament, the link with the Swedish crown was, however, increasingly resented. Composers such as Edvard Grieg and writers such as Henrik Ibsen made Norwegians proud of their own culture.

Father of Australia

Sir Harry Parkes (1815-96) urged the Australian colonies to join together as a **federation** but died before his goal was achieved. In 1867, he said:

'With our splendid harbour, our beautifully situated city, our vast territories, all our varied and inexhaustible natural wealth, if we don't convert our colony into a great and prosperous nation, it will be a miracle of error for which we will have to answer as for a gigantic sin.'

In 1905 the Norwegian Parliament voted to dissolve the union. After three months of discussion Sweden accepted this, and Norway and Sweden achieved a peaceful separation. The Norwegians invited a Danish prince to become their king. Finland was part of Sweden until it was conquered by Russia in 1809. The Finns resisted Russian culture through their language, their Protestantism and pride in their national composer, Jean Sibelius. They became a separate nation again in 1917.

A new state for the oldest nation?

Since Roman times, Jewish people had been scattered through many countries, sometimes prospering but often facing persecution. By the late nineteenth century, half of the world's ten million Jews lived under Russian rule. From the 1880s they suffered repeated pogroms – violent, anti-Jewish riots – which led many to emigrate. In 1895 Theodor Herzl, a Jewish journalist and playwright living in Vienna, wrote *Der Judenstaat* (The Jewish State). In it he argued that Jews should have their own independent country where they could be free and secure. Herzl promoted this belief, known as Zionism, at the first World Zionist Conference which he organized in 1897. Half a century later, Zionism became a reality with the foundation of Israel in 1948.

The Scandinavian people retain distinct and separate national identities. These children are taking part in a procession to celebrate Norway's national day.

Empires into Nations

Nationalism during the nineteenth century was largely confined to Europe and mainly took the form of opposition to neighbouring peoples. During the twentieth century, nationalism extended beyond Europe and concerned various peoples' opposition to rule by Westerners.

In 1901 a young British MP, Winston Churchill (1874–1965), predicted: 'The wars of the peoples will be more terrible than those of kings.… A European war can only end in the ruin of the vanquished and the hardly less fatal… exhaustion of the conquerors.'

An explosion of nationalism

France's defeat by Prussia in 1870–1 (see page 27) cost it the two eastern provinces of Alsace and Lorraine. This loss was a tremendous blow to national pride. French nationalists dreamed of a war of revenge to recover the provinces. Alsace and Lorraine became part of the new German Empire, which quickly grew into the richest and most powerful state in Europe. France allied itself with Russia. Germany therefore drew closer to Austria–Hungary as a counter-weight to Russia. Britain, alarmed at Germany's decision to build a great navy, drew closer to France.

Nationalist hopes and rivalries were most dangerous in the **Balkan** region

The fever of war

The Austrian writer Stefan Zweig (1881-1942) described the atmosphere in the Austrian capital, Vienna, on the outbreak of the First World War:

'I found the city in a tumult... parades in the streets, flags, ribbons and music burst forth everywhere, young recruits were marching triumphantly, their faces lighting up at the cheering... hundreds of thousands felt... that they belonged together... that they were participating in world history. All differences of class, rank and language were flooded over.... Each individual... was part of the people and... had been given meaning.... They did not know war.... They still saw it through their schoolbooks and paintings in museums... a wild, manly adventure... and the young people were honestly afraid they might miss this most wonderful and exciting experience of their lives... that is why they shouted and sang in the trains that carried them to the slaughter.'

of south-eastern Europe. Like Greece (see page 22), the states of Romania, Bulgaria, Serbia and Montenegro had won their independence from the multinational **Ottoman Empire**. The multinational **Austro-Hungarian Empire** became alarmed at the growth of Serbia. It feared that Serbs still living under Austro-Hungarian rule in Bosnia-Herzegovina might try to break away.

In June 1914 the heir to the Austro-Hungarian throne was assassinated while visiting Sarajevo, the capital of Bosnia-Herzegovina, on Serbia's national day. The assassin was a young Serb, living in Bosnia. Although the Serbian government denied any involvement, the murder gave Austria-Hungary (with Germany's backing) an excuse to invade Serbia. Russia's decision to aid Serbia then caused the interlocking alliance system to drag in France and Britain (known as the Allied Powers). Italy, although allied to Germany and Austria-Hungary (known as the Central Powers), stayed neutral at first. Bulgaria and the Ottomans sided with the Central Powers. This conflict would become the First World War.

Serbian student nationalist Gavrilo Princip is seized after assassinating Archduke Franz Ferdinand of Austria-Hungary on 28 June 1914.

The First World War

Socialists in Germany, France and Britain protested that working men, whatever their country of origin, had far more in common with each other than with the quarrels that divided their rulers. But the First World War showed that the appeal of nationalism was far more powerful than the brotherhood of working men. When the British government appealed for soldiers, 750,000 men volunteered in a month, far more than the army could train, arm or even clothe in uniform.

The USA was provoked into joining the war by German submarine attacks on neutral, especially American, shipping. US President Woodrow Wilson (1856-1924) had pledged to keep out of the war, but in 1916 declared: 'the nation's honour is dearer than the nation's comfort'. In 1917 the USA joined the increasingly exhausted Allied Powers, just as Russia was slipping into chaos and revolution. Wilson claimed that America wanted nothing for itself but to punish German aggression and to free oppressed nations by granting them self-rule. The supply of fresh American forces led to the defeat of the Central Powers. It also meant that Wilson was able to dominate the post-war Paris peace conference.

Defeat smashed the multi-ethnic empires of Russia, Austria-Hungary and the Ottomans. As Russia collapsed into revolution, its former provinces of Poland, Finland, Lithuania, Latvia and Estonia declared themselves independent. Austria-Hungary was split into a separate Austria and Hungary. The Czechs and Slovaks were joined together to make a new state – Czechoslovakia. The former Balkan provinces of the empire – Slovenia, Croatia and Bosnia-Herzegovina – joined Serbia and Montenegro to create Yugoslavia. But none of these arrangements were as neat as they looked on a map.

Ireland reborn – mostly

Ireland's situation illustrated the problem of divided loyalties. 250,000 Irishmen served in the British army during the First World War. At the same time, in 1916, with German weapons and support, 2,000 Irish nationalist volunteers launched an unsuccessful Easter Rising in Dublin against British rule. The British crushed the rebels in a week, during which 794 civilians and 521 police and troops were killed. Then the British government made a major political mistake by executing fifteen of the leaders. This turned the rebels into martyrs and rallied widespread Irish support for the nationalist cause.

Ireland became increasingly ungovernable as nationalists waged a **guerrilla** war against British forces. In 1922 the British government agreed to separate the country in two, keeping only the six Protestant-dominated counties of Ulster and recognizing the other 26 counties as an independent Irish Free State (now the Republic of Ireland).

Peace, Bread, Land – in 1917, the communist revolutionary Lenin tempted the war-weary subjects of the Tsar with the promise of a new beginning.

The post-war peace conferences only partly accepted the principle of **self-determination**. Not all Hungarians were in the new Hungary. Some found themselves under Polish, others under Romanian, rule. Large numbers of Germans were in Czechoslovakia or Poland or Lithuania. Koreans protesting against Japan's take-over of Korea were ignored, as was the **Pan-African** Congress which wanted freedom from European **colonial rule**.

Fascism

Italy, which joined the Allied Powers in 1915 to gain **territory** from Austria–Hungary, lost 300,000 men in the First World War and gained very little. National frustration joined with the fear that the **communist** take-over of Russia (1917-22) would turn into revolution throughout Europe. This sense of unease built support for a new extreme, nationalist movement led by an ex-journalist, Benito Mussolini (1883-1945). The movement was known as **fascism**.

Mussolini came to power in 1922 but gradually built up a **dictatorship** in Italy. Meanwhile in defeated Germany, ex-soldier Adolf Hitler (1889-1945), an Austrian by birth and an admirer of Mussolini, recruited supporters to his own form of fascism, called Nazism.

Both Italian fascism and German Nazism promised to set their nations on a path to glory and prosperity by waging war against internal and external enemies. These extreme forms of nationalism suppressed opposition in the name of the unity, discipline and sacrifice they demanded. Mussolini thought in terms of a colonial empire in Africa, and brutally conquered Ethiopia in 1936. Hitler's main aim was to unite all Germans under his leadership in a single state and use it to conquer a vast empire in the east, reducing Slav peoples to slavery and, eventually, to extinction.

On top of his podium Benito Mussolini gives the fascist salute. Fascist governments relied on rituals, slogans, uniforms and propaganda to build up support.

The Soviet Union

The communist revolution in Russia led to the creation of a Union of Soviet Socialist Republics (USSR, also known as the Soviet Union) out of the wreckage of the Russian Empire. In theory, its different **republics** were to be equal with one another. They were to be bound together by the shared communist ideal of a universal brotherhood of working peoples, which extended beyond national loyalties. In practice, the USSR was dominated by Russia and the Russian language. It allowed and even encouraged national minorities to express their culture in harmless forms, such as folk dancing, but ruthlessly oppressed religion and any challenge to its power.

Mustafa Kemal (1880-1938)

An Ottoman army officer, Kemal fought brilliantly during the First World War and defeated a Greek invasion afterwards to become a national hero. He saw the break-up of the Ottoman Empire as the chance to build a new Turkey out of its ruins. As first president of the Turkish republic, he modernized the Turkish language and education, built up industry, gave women the vote and encouraged European-style clothes and manners. A new capital, Ankara, was built in the Turkish heartland. All Turks were ordered: 'Be Proud You are Turkish!' and were instructed to take a second name. Kemal chose Ataturk – 'Father Turk'. Although he crushed opposition to his reforms, Ataturk was respected as a great patriot. His picture is still seen everywhere in Turkey.

Turkish leader Mustafa Kemal promoted change by his own example, always wearing Western suits or uniforms, rather than traditional Muslim clothes.

A world at war

In 1938 German troops **annexed** Hitler's homeland, Austria. Hitler then demanded that the three million Germans living in Czechoslovakia come under German rule. Rather than fight, Britain and France agreed that German-speaking territory should be detached from Czechoslovakia. Czechoslovakia had no option but to accept this.

In March 1939 Hitler annexed the rest of Czechoslovakia and seized the former Prussian port of Memel from Lithuania. Seeing that Hitler could not be bought off, Britain and France then guaranteed to help Poland if Germany attacked it. When German troops invaded Poland shortly afterwards, in September 1939, the Second World War began.

Invading German armies posed as 'national liberators' in Slovakia (where the Slovaks resented the Czechs), Croatia (where the Croats hated the Serbs) and the Ukraine (where the Ukrainians hated the Russians). The Germans allowed them to set up their own governments. In theory these were independent, in practice they were just a way of organizing soldiers and supplies to support the German war effort.

Hitler reviewing uniformed Nazi supporters. Parades and rallies were a dramatic way of demonstrating to the public the strength of support for Nazism.

Japan, meanwhile, took advantage of the defeats suffered by Britain, France and the Netherlands in Europe to conquer their **colonies** in South-East Asia, likewise posing as a national liberator and declaring 'Asia for the Asians'. Although the Japanese did help local nationalists, in reality their occupation of former European colonies proved far crueller than colonial rule.

German troops invading Poland in 1939. Germany's search for 'Lebensraum' (living space) in Eastern Europe finally ended with the displacement of 12,000,000 Germans as refugees.

In defeating the German invasion, USSR forces annexed the independent Baltic republics of Estonia, Latvia and Lithuania. Following the defeat of Germany in 1945, the USSR set up a communist government in the eastern part of Germany that its troops controlled. It also helped local communists take power in Poland, Czechoslovakia, Hungary, Romania and Bulgaria. In Albania and Yugoslavia, local communist fighters took power after defeating the invading Italians and Germans.

Decolonization

The long-term effect of the Second World War was to weaken the British, French and Dutch empires so that they were forced to abandon their colonies. The war had cost them huge sums of money and their peoples were more interested in rebuilding their lives at home than in fighting to regain or hold on to colonies abroad. From the 1940s to the 1960s, throughout Asia and Africa, these colonies became independent states.

Britain's Indian Empire split into India, Pakistan and a Buddhist Burma (Myanmar). The decision of Kashmir, a Muslim state under a Hindu ruler, to join India has led to conflict between India and Pakistan ever since. In Palestine, Britain failed to balance the demands of Jewish immigrants with the rights of local Arabs. The Jewish people were simply left to fight, successfully, for an independent Israel in 1948.

France fought to hang on to Vietnam, until defeat in 1954. France also held on to Algeria until 1962, when it quit after a war costing 500,000 lives. In Indonesia, the Dutch were likewise beaten by a nationalist guerrilla campaign, and recognized Indonesian independence in 1949.

In much of Africa, the withdrawal of a colonial power sometimes removed the most important factor uniting its former subjects. Leaders of new nations competed for power by appealing to tribal or

The Htoo twins

The Burmese account for two-thirds of the population of Myanmar. The largest of many minorities is the Karen people, some of whom have been fighting for a separate Karen state ever since Myanmar became independent from British rule in 1948. Burmese army counter-attacks have forced tens of thousands of Karens over the border into refugee camps in Thailand. By 1997, only a few thousand Karen guerrillas were left fighting. Then a band of 200, calling itself God's Army, began to win against the Burmese under the leadership of twelve-year-old twins, Luther and Johnny Htoo. Their followers thought they had magic powers which protected them in battle and guaranteed victory. They obeyed their orders not to swear, drink, gamble or eat pork. In 2001, however, the Htoo twins gave up fighting and fled to a refugee camp in Thailand.

regional loyalties. This resulted in civil wars in such states as Congo, Angola, Mozambique, Sudan and Nigeria (see page 53).

Throughout Asia and Africa, movements for national independence promised equality, planning and modernization for all **citizens** of the future new nations. But these promises were rarely kept. The new **post-colonial** nations were usually desperately short of trained managers, doctors, teachers, etc. and often depended for their prosperity on the success and price of a few key crops or raw materials. Unrealistic ambitions, corruption and ancient rivalries between ethnic and religious groups have often combined to produce instability in such nations.

Lord Mountbatten, the last British viceroy, is cheered as India achieves independence in 1948.

Mohandas Gandhi (1869-1948)

Gandhi trained as a lawyer in England and settled in South Africa, where his struggle for the rights of Indian immigrants made him known as Mahatma – 'Great Soul'. Returning to India in 1914, Gandhi accepted British rule until a massacre of peaceful demonstrators in 1919 led him to launch a movement of non-violent resistance. His methods included strikes, non-payment of taxes, refusal to buy British goods and hunger strikes. Gandhi hoped the common struggle against British rule would unite India's Hindu majority and its Muslim minority into one people. He was deeply saddened when British rule ended with separation into a Hindu-dominated India and a Muslim-dominated Pakistan, and the loss of half a million lives in Hindu-Muslim riots. Gandhi was shot dead by a Hindu for his sympathy with Muslims. Gandhi's non-violent methods were an inspiration for the US civil rights movement of the 1950s.

Nationalism and Communism

To many of its followers, **communism** seemed to offer the promise of an idea that was bigger and better than nationalism. It promised a world in which peoples everywhere would work together for the benefit of all. But, in practice, **communist** governments often manipulated nationalist feelings to create hatred and fear between peoples.

From the 1940s until the break-up of the USSR in 1989-91, world politics was dominated by a confrontation known as the Cold War. On one side stood the USA and its allies, on the other the USSR and its allies. In theory, communism promised a future world in which the brotherhood of working people would make national frontiers meaningless. In practice, communist states usually imposed tight border security to prevent their peoples leaving and to control contact with the outside world. Nationalist resistance to communism led to failed uprisings in East Germany in 1953, in Hungary in 1956 and in Czechoslovakia in 1968. These uprisings were suppressed by Soviet armed forces, and as a result thousands were driven into **exile**.

In 1968, Russian tanks enter Prague to crush Czech reforms for greater freedom. The invading troops were bewildered when they were not welcomed.

Cult of personality

In theory, communist states, inspired by the same ideas, should have been very similar. In practice, they kept distinct national characteristics. Communism stressed that all working people were of equal value. The strictly controlled art and literature of communist states presented the workers as heroic figures in paintings, posters, films and ballets. But several communist states also presented their leader as a figure of genius – for example, as a great writer, thinker, teacher and commander – whose picture and statue were seen everywhere and whose sayings and doings filled newspapers, TV programmes and schoolbooks.

This 'cult of personality' began in the USSR with the leader of the revolution, Lenin (1870-1924), and reached its height there under his successor, Stalin (1879-1953). It was copied by the Chinese leader Mao Zedong (1893-1976) and to a lesser extent in Vietnam by Ho Chi Minh (1890-1969). The island of Cuba has been dominated by its communist leader, Fidel Castro (1926-) ever since he took power in 1959. The cult of personality was most evident in Romania with Nicolae Ceausescu (1918-89), in Albania with Enver Hoxha (1908-85) and, above all, in North Korea (see box below).

Fidel Castro has ruled Cuba ever since seizing power in 1959. His brother is his deputy.

Like father, like son

The cult of personality became most extreme in North Korea. 'Great Leader' Kim Il Sung (1912-94) was presented as the hero who had freed Korea from Japanese rule and transformed the country into a modern industrial power. In reality his spending on weapons and grand buildings brought the country to ruin. But this did not prevent his son, 'Dear Leader' Kim Jong Il (1942-) from succeeding him. Seven years of famine in the 1990s killed two million people, but North Korea remains isolated from the rest of the world and under Kim's control.

Marshal Tito successfully balanced the rivalries of Serbs, Croats and other nations in Yugoslavia.

Although communist states claimed to be co-operating unselfishly with each other to build a better world, in reality they behaved according to their own national interests. In 1949 communists took power in China and relied heavily on the USSR to help them build up modern industries. But within ten years China had quarrelled with the USSR about how a communist country should be run and the USSR withdrew its experts and support. The two countries increasingly became rivals rather than partners.

When the USSR allied itself to India and supplied it with weapons, China did the same for India's rival, Pakistan. North Vietnam relied on Chinese weapons and support to re-unite North and South Vietnam by force between 1954 and 1975. When re-united Vietnam invaded neighbouring Cambodia in 1978, China disapproved and punished it by devastating Vietnam's northern frontier in 1979. Vietnam therefore switched to the USSR for its weapons, providing use of a former US naval base in exchange.

Nationalisms revived

Under the ex-**guerrilla** commander Marshal Tito (1892-1980), Yugoslavia refused to follow the USSR in its dealings with other nations, traded freely with non-communist countries and welcomed foreign tourists. Unlike most communist governments, it allowed factories and farms to run themselves. Internal politics was based on a careful balancing act as Tito played off different national groups – Serbs, Croats, Bosnians, Slovenes – against each other. This system outlasted Tito's rule by a decade, but ended in catastrophe as communism was abandoned in favour of re-establishing separate national groupings. Slovenia and Macedonia broke away from Yugoslavia almost bloodlessly. But when Croatia in 1991 and Bosnia-Herzegovina in 1992 aimed at independence,

Serbia began a war costing 250,000 lives before it accepted that the former Yugoslavia had been reduced to itself and Montenegro.

In 1989-91 the break-up of the USSR led to nationalist revivals throughout Eastern Europe, from the Baltic to Hungary, as communist governments were overthrown. It also brought about the reunification of East and West Germany into one country and the creation of new, independent states in the Caucasus and Central Asia.

In 1989 the Berlin Wall – symbol of Germany's division into West and East – was finally torn down.

A nation suppressed

Tibet's identity rests on its language and a distinctive form of Buddhism. The nation's spiritual leader is the Dalai Lama. In 1720, the Chinese incorporated Tibet into their empire but did not try to impose Chinese culture. When the Chinese Empire collapsed in 1911, Tibet declared its independence and expelled all Chinese. After the communist take-over of China in 1949, the new Chinese government laid claim to the ancient borders of its empire and invaded Tibet in 1950-1.

The influx of Chinese soldiers and migrants and the suppression of Buddhism provoked a Tibetan uprising in 1959. The Dalai Lama and more than 50,000 followers were forced into exile in India, where they remain. In theory, there is an **autonomous** local government, staffed and headed by Tibetans. In practice, power rests with the Chinese Communist Party, headed by the Chinese, with all major decisions approved in Beijing. The Chinese continue to rely on military occupation to enforce their rule. The exiled Dalai Lama has said that, because Tibet is poor, it would be better off as part of a rapidly prospering country like China. But he wants the Chinese to withdraw their soldiers and leave the Tibetans free to follow their religion and their own way of life. The plight of Tibetan refugees and of Tibet itself has attracted the concern of Westerners, such as pop star Bono and actor Richard Gere, who campaign against Chinese human rights abuses.

Beyond the Nation State

Conflict – both within and between countries – has often occurred because the supposed boundaries of nations and the actual frontiers of states are not the same. Different nations may disagree about where their frontiers are. This has led to repeated challenges from some states to the very existence of others. Argentina lays claim to the Falkland Islands (Las Malvinas) which have been occupied by British settlers since 1833. In 1982 Argentina invaded the Falklands and was forced out by a British task force at the cost of 1,500 lives. In 1990 Iraqi dictator Saddam Hussein (1937-) invaded oil-rich Kuwait, claiming that it was really a 'lost province' of Iraq. The USA led a coalition that restored Kuwaiti independence at a cost of 50,000-100,000 Iraqi lives.

Another type of challenge can arise from movements that want to unite existing states in the name of a larger nation. Such movements include Pan-Slavism, Pan-Arabism, Pan-Africanism and Pan-Europeanism.

Kuwait following the Gulf War of 1991. The Iraqi leader Saddam Hussein claimed Kuwait as a 'lost' province of Iraq. He invaded, but was driven back by an alliance led by the United States. Saddam instructed the retreating Iraqi army to set fire to Kuwaiti oil wells, causing great devastation.

Pan-Slavism

Pan-Slavism was the belief that speakers of Slavic languages, such as Russian, Czech and Bulgarian, make up a distinct civilization and should form a **confederation** of states. During the nineteenth century Pan-Slavism provided an excuse for Russia to interfere in the politics of the **Balkans**. In 1876 Bulgaria, then an Ottoman province, rose in a revolt that was brutally suppressed. In 1877-8 Russia fought and defeated the Ottomans, partly to show Pan-Slav support for the Bulgarians, partly to continue its long-term aim of weakening the **Ottoman Empire**. Bulgaria became a kingdom with an imported German monarch. It became fully independent in 1908 and other Ottoman Balkan **territories** became independent as Romania, Serbia and Montenegro.

Pan-Arabism

Pan-Arabism, favoured by some Arab Muslims, ignores the fact that the Arab world also contains many Berbers, Turks and Kurds (all of whom are Muslims but not Arabs), as well as Jews and Christian Arabs, Armenians and Copts. Attempts have been made to unite two existing Arab states as a first step towards the creation of an Arab superstate. But these have failed in practice. Egypt and Syria, which do not even have a common border, agreed to merge in 1958 but angrily proclaimed their separation in 1961. Colonel Qaddafi of Libya has repeatedly offered mergers with other Arab states, but none has been tried seriously.

Even if these neighbouring states did unite successfully and national minorities could be reassured that their rights would be respected, there remains the problem that some states have very different political systems. For example, Syria, Yemen and Algeria are **republics**, whereas Jordan, Morocco, Oman, Kuwait, the Emirates and Saudi Arabia have traditional monarchies.

The League of Arab States

One positive outcome of Pan-Arabism, however, was the formation of the League of Arab States in 1945. This has promoted useful co-operation between states in such areas as telecommunications, postal services and banking. But the League has been divided over attitudes to the USSR, Iraq's 1990 invasion of Kuwait, extreme Islamic movements and the best way to support Palestinians in Israel.

Pan-Africanism

Pan-Africanism grew out of a series of six congresses of African intellectuals and **political activists** that were held in cities outside Africa between 1900 and 1945. These congresses pressed and planned for the independence of African **colonies** from European rule. In calling the first Conference of Independent African States in Ghana in 1958, the Ghanaian leader, Kwame Nkrumah (1909-72), hoped to launch a further movement that would unite the continent under his leadership. For a few years Ghana's prosperity enabled him to cut a big figure on the world stage. But Ghana was a small country and soon ruined by Nkrumah's extravagant dreams to make it a modern industrial power overnight. Nigeria, Ghana's oil-rich West African neighbour, was scarcely likely to put itself under Ghanaian leadership when it had only just got its own independence from British rule. It was even less likely that former French-speaking colonies would be willing to join an English-speaking community.

A more practical beginning was the foundation in 1963 of the Organization of African Unity (OAU). This has tried to settle disputes and promote co-operation between its 53 member states. At a summit meeting of the OAU in July 2002 its members voted to re-establish it as the African Union, organized along the same lines as the European Union (EU).

Pan-Europeanism

Supporters of the European Union, who hope that one day its members will merge into a European superstate, can be seen as believers in a form of pan-Europeanism. The reality is that the newly independent Eastern European countries that are eager to join the EU have only recently escaped from suppression by **communist** governments. They want to join the EU for reasons of prosperity and security – not in order to give up their national identities.

Prior nations

Some peoples claim to have been nations since before the modern idea of nationalism emerged. But it is not clear whether in the United States, for example, Native Americans should be thought of as a single nation or as a group of separate nations, such as the Iroquois. Similarly, are Canada's First Nations, Australia's Aboriginals or New Zealand's Maoris one people or separate peoples? Before white settlement, each of these separate peoples spoke different languages and fought among themselves. But some argue that the common experience of being pushed aside and then left behind has given **native peoples** a common history more powerful in uniting them than whatever divided them in the past. In practice, however, these are not nationalist groups because most of their members want fair treatment within their existing state rather than a separate, independent one.

Uniting Europe

'We must free ourselves from thinking in terms of nation states.... The countries of Western Europe are no longer in a position to protect themselves individually; not one of them is any longer in a position to salvage Europe's culture.'

Konrad Adenauer (1876-1967), chancellor of West Germany, 1953.

In 1992 Native Americans used the 500th anniversary of Columbus's arrival in the Americas as an opportunity to protest for more rights.

Countries in conflict

Some nationalist movements aim to break out of existing states in order to achieve independence. In the Caucasus, for example, Abkhazia and South Ossetia are seeking to break away from Georgia. Nagorno-Karabakh wants to break away from Azerbaijan and Chechnya is fighting an occupying Russian army.

The following are examples of peoples who challenged an existing state to establish themselves as new, independent nations, hoping to achieve greater justice and security for themselves. They also show how nationalism can lead to the destruction of human life on a great scale.

Small nations have often successfully defied powerful empires – at a price. Here Chechen fighters take on Russian troops in January 1995.

Biafra

In 1960, Nigeria became independent from British rule. Its three regions were dominated by different peoples – the Christian and Muslim speakers of Yoruba in the west, the Muslim speakers of Hausa in the north and the Christian speakers of Ibo in the east. The discovery of oil off the coast of the eastern region meant it could grow much richer than the other regions as an independent state, keeping the oil wealth to itself. In January 1966, a group of Ibo army officers murdered Nigeria's prime minister and the chief ministers of the northern and western regions. In September, tens of thousands of Ibo living in the northern region were massacred by mobs. A million people fled back to the Ibo homeland, which began to expel non-Ibo peoples. In May 1967 the eastern region, led by Colonel Ojukwu, declared that it was breaking away from Nigeria to become the independent Republic of Biafra. A three-year civil war followed, bringing starvation and disease, which cost up to 1,000,000 lives until the devastated eastern region was forced to abandon its bid for freedom.

Bangladesh

When British rule over India ended in 1947, the two large areas in which Muslims made up the majority of the population formed a separate new state of Pakistan. The two areas were 1,500 kilometres apart. West Pakistan was bigger and richer, and its people spoke Urdu. East Pakistan had a larger, Bengali-speaking, population. The people of East Pakistan believed that West Pakistan was taking more than its fair share of taxes and top jobs. In 1971, East Pakistan declared its independence as Bangladesh, meaning 'Free Bengal'. When armed forces loyal to West Pakistan resisted, it led to a civil war in which the Bengalis were aided by the powerful Indian army. It suited India to divide its neighbour into two smaller states, so an independent Bangladesh was born.

East Timor

Until 1974, Portugal controlled the eastern half of the island of Timor. However a military takeover in Portugal itself offered the Timorese the chance to seize their independence. After a brief civil war between pro and anti independence groups, East Timor declared its independence. But it was then invaded and taken over by neighbouring Indonesia. The Indonesians imported settlers to swamp the Catholic, Portuguese-speaking Timorese with a Muslim, Indonesian-speaking majority. Tension continued until the deadlock was unexpectedly broken by the fall of the government of General Suharto in Indonesia. To resolve the Timor problem Suharto's successor in 1999 allowed a **plebiscite** in which 78.5 per cent of Timorese opted for independence. The local Indonesian military then armed Indonesian settlers to fight this decision. Thousands of people were killed and 250,000 Timorese were driven into temporary **exile**. In September 1999, a UN military force under Australian command restored order. A UN temporary government then organized the move to full independence, achieved on 20 May 2002.

Sri Lanka

Three-quarters of the people of Sri Lanka are Sinhalese-speakers and the majority are Buddhist. There is also a Tamil-speaking, mostly Hindu minority. Since the mid-1980s militia forces known as the Tamil Tigers have fought to establish a Tamil homeland – Tamil Eelam – in Jaffna, a peninsula at the north-eastern tip of Sri Lanka. More than 60,000 have died in the conflict, 100,000 Tamils have fled to India and 200,000 to the West. Tiger militias have recruited hundreds of fighters, some as young as twelve, in the refugee camps. In February 2002, the government and rebels agreed to a ceasefire to pave the way for peace talks.

Tamil Tigers in training in Sri Lanka in 1995. Some recruits were as young as twelve.

Kurdistan

There are more than 20 million Kurds living in Kurdistan, a mountainous area of land split between Turkey, Iraq, Iran and Syria. The Kurds do not share a common language or religion but have fought for an independent state because of the oppression they have suffered at the hands of others, especially Iraq and Turkey. Iraq has executed perhaps as many as 100,000 Kurdish men. Iraq's defeat in the 1991 Gulf War led to an Iraqi-Kurdish uprising. It failed and led to two million Kurds being without a home. As a result, the USA and its allies declared and successfully protected with air patrols a 'safe haven' in northern Iraq. Before the war in Iraq in 2003 this area was effectively self-governing, but the future for the Kurds in post-Saddam Iraq remains uncertain.

Nationalism – Today and Tomorrow

Nationalism still fuels conflicts within developed nations, and not only those with a colonial past.

Spain

Two million Basques live in north-east Spain and 200,000 live in south-west France. The Basque language, Euskara, is one that has no similarities with any other known language. The Basques claim to be directly descended from the Cro-Magnon cave dwellers who lived in their region 20,000 years ago; but they have never had an independent state of their own. And the name they give to their homeland – Euskadi, meaning 'Euskara-speakers united' – was only invented in the late nineteenth century.

In Spain the dictator General Franco (1892-1975) abolished the regional governments of Catalonia and the Basque provinces and suppressed the Catalan and Basque languages. Following his death, the country was divided into seventeen self-governing regions. This satisfied the Catalans, but not an extremist Basque minority.

For Basque nationalists, language is the basis of Basque identity, although only a third of all Basques actually speak it. Since 1979, Basque has been taught in schools, so now 90 per cent of Basque children are learning the language. In 1980 a Basque Parliament was elected to govern the provinces of Vizcaya (Bizkaia), Alava (Araba) and Guipuzcoa (Gipuzkoa).

Within this region, Basque is recognized as an official language alongside Spanish. Since 1968 a Basque **separatist** organization, ETA (Euskadi ta Askatasuna,

Following the flag – a Basque nationalist demonstration.

meaning 'Basque Nation and Liberty'), has used terrorism to press for a separate Basque state. More than 800 people have been killed, including a prime minister of Spain. ETA may have fewer than forty active terrorists, though many more supporters are willing to provide shelter, supplies or information.

France
French government became highly **centralized** after the revolution in 1789. The armed forces, courts, schools, etc. were required to use the French language and ignore local languages, such as Breton, Provencal, Alsatian or Corsican. Until the 1980s officials could refuse to register the births of children who had been given Breton or Basque first names. Since then, official attitudes have reversed so that government now supports the preservation and teaching of these languages.

Regionalist movements in France challenge the power of the central government. This has erupted in violence in Corsica, with the murder of some 220 French officials and police since 1976. Many people in France fear that conceding any sort of special status to Corsica – let alone full independence – will only encourage other minorities, such as Bretons and Basques, to raise demands, threatening the unity of the French state.

Canada
The first Europeans to settle in Canada were French. Under British rule after 1763 Canada became overwhelmingly English-speaking. French-speakers remained concentrated in Quebec, where change was slow in a society of small farmers, which was dominated by the Catholic Church. During the twentieth century, as towns and modern industry grew, they did so under the control of English-speakers in Quebec.

Between 1960 and 1966 the Liberal Party took control of the Quebec provincial government and set up state-owned enterprises headed by French-speakers. Under the leadership of the Parti Quebecois (PQ), founded in 1968, laws were passed in Quebec giving local preference to French. Canada's federal government agreed to make French equal with English as a national language and pledged to protect the rights of French-speakers outside Quebec. The PQ continued to insist that Quebec was more than just a 'distinct society' – it was a nation. In 1980 Quebec voters rejected a call for complete independence from Canada. In 1995, 49.5 per cent voted in favour of independence. Clearly more Quebecois were becoming in favour of separation.

Bloc Quebecois leader Lucien Bouchard waves to his supporters during a 'Yes' rally in favour of independence in Montreal, Canada, on 25 October 1995.

No solution in sight?

Two other nationalist confrontations seem to be without solution. In Northern Ireland, which is still ruled by Britain, the British and Irish governments have agreed to create a power-sharing system. This means that the nationalist/**republican** minority, many of whom wish to unite it with the Republic of Ireland, and the unionist/loyalist majority, who mostly want to remain part of the UK both have a part in local government. Both British and Irish governments have also pledged that no change will be made without a clear vote in favour by a majority of the population of Northern Ireland.

In the Middle East, Israel and Palestine remain locked in a cycle of violence. Palestinians forced from their homeland during Israel's 1948 war of independence use terrorism to demand an independent state in Gaza and the West Bank area. Israel uses its armed forces to punish terrorism and continues to build new settlements in former Palestinian territory.

A Palestinian woman and her child watch as Israeli forces use bulldozers to demolish Palestinian homes in retaliation for terrorist attacks in April 2002.

Leading Western powers and the main Arab states agree that Palestinians must have a state and Israel's right to exist within secure borders must be accepted. After so much hatred has built up between Israelis and Palestinians, the problem is for either side to trust the other enough to accept a peaceful solution.

Working together

Many of the world's problems, such as the environment, finance, drugs, AIDs and terrorism, cannot be confined within national boundaries and can only be tackled effectively by nations working together. The increasing movement of populations and global access to information through the Internet challenges the notion of fixed national identities. The likelihood is that we shall all increasingly learn to live across frontiers, rather than simply within them.

Nationalism as a habit

'The established nations are those states that have confidence in their own continuity.... The political leaders of such nations – whether France, the USA, the UK or New Zealand – are not typically termed nationalists. However... in so many little ways, the citizenry are daily reminded of their national place in a world of nations... this reminding is so familiar that it is not consciously registered... nationalism is not a flag which is being consciously waved with fervent passion; it is the flag hanging unnoticed on the public building.'

Michael Billig, Professor of Social Science, University of Loughborough, UK, 1995.

Date List

c. 1745   The first national anthem 'God Save the King' (Britain)

1776   American Declaration of Independence

1789   French Revolution and Declaration of the Rights of Man and the Citizen

1807–8   Fichte's 'Addresses to the German Nation'

1815   Defeat of Napoleon

1830   Revolution in France sparks off nationalist risings in Belgium (successful), Italian cities (failed) and Poland (failed)

1848   Revolutions throughout Europe (failed)

1853   Japan forced into contact with the outside world

1859   France and Piedmont liberate Italian territory from Austrian rule

1863   Failed nationalist rising in Poland

1866   Prussia defeats Austria. Venetia passes to Italy.

1867   British colonies in North America join together as the self-governing Dominion of Canada

1870–1   Franco-Prussian war leads to establishment of the German empire

1877–8   Russo-Turkish war establishes independence of Serbia, Montenegro and Romania

1884   Berlin conference establishes colonial boundaries in Africa. Gaelic Athletic Association founded.

1885   Indian National Congress founded

1897   First World Zionist Congress held in Basle, Switzerland

1900   Pan-African Congress held in London

1901   Commonwealth of Australia established by former British colonies

1905   Norway breaks away peacefully from Sweden

1914–18   First World War

1916   Irish Nationalist Easter Rising in Dublin

1917–22   Russian Revolution and civil war establishes the Union of Soviet Socialist Republics (USSR, Soviet Union). Former Russian provinces reclaim independence as Poland, Finland, Estonia, Latvia and Lithuania.

1919   Paris Peace Conference; Pan-African Congress held in Paris

1920   Foundation of the League of Nations

1921   Pan-African Congress held in London

1922   Mussolini comes to power in Italy. Partition of Ireland.

1923   Pan-African Congress held in London

1927   Pan-African Congress held in New York

1928   Scottish National Party established

1931   USA adopts 'The Star-Spangled Banner' as its national anthem

1933   Hitler comes to power in Germany

1939–45   Second World War

1945   United Nations establishes Pan-African Congress held in Manchester. Arab League founded.

1947   Partition of India and Pakistan

1948   Establishment of the State of Israel

1949   The Netherlands recognizes independence of Indonesia. Communists take power in China.

1950   Israel's Law of Return guarantees citizenship for overseas Jews

1953   Failed anti-Communist uprising in East Germany

1954   France recognizes independence of Vietnam

1956   Failed anti-Communist uprising in Hungary

1957   Gold Coast (Ghana) becomes the

Resources

first British colony in Africa to achieve independence. Rome treaties establish the European Economic Community, forerunner of the European Union.

1959 Fidel Castro takes power in Cuba. Tibetan uprising against Chinese rule.

1962 France recognizes independence of Algeria

1963 Organization of African Unity founded

1967–70 Biafran breakaway from Nigeria defeated

1968 Failed anti-Communist uprising in Czechoslovakia. Parti Quebecois founded.

1971 East Pakistan breaks away to become Bangladesh

1975 North and South Vietnam reunited

1989–91 Breakup of the USSR

1992–4 Bosnia-Herzegovina fights for independence

1993 Czechoslovakia splits peacefully into the Czech Republic and Slovakia

1997 Scotland and Wales vote for devolution

2002 East Timor becomes independent

Encyclopaedia of Nationalism, A. Motyl, Academic Press, 2000

National Identity, A. D. Smith, Penguin, 1991

Nations and Nationalism, Ernest Gellner, Blackwell, 1983

Nations and Nationalism Since 1780: Programme, Myth and Reality, Eric Hobsbawm, Cambridge University Press, 1990

The Oxford Companion to the Politics of the World, Joel Krieger, Oxford University Press, 2001

The Oxford Dictionary of Political Biography, Denis Kavanagh, Oxford University Press, 1998

The Penguin Dictionary of Politics, David Robertson, Penguin, 1993

Glossary

annex

take over a territory.

anti-imperialism

opposition to being ruled by a foreign country as part of its empire.

atheist

someone who does not believe in God or gods.

Austro-Hungarian Empire

multi-ethnic empire of central and south-eastern Europe ruled by members of the Habsburg family until its collapse in 1918. The politically powerful Austrians and Hungarians dominated a dozen other peoples including Czechs, Slovaks, Slovenes, Croats.

autocratic

rule by single person.

autonomy

self-rule, especially in matters of culture, such as language.

Balkans

mountainous region of south-eastern Europe, between Hungary and Greece.

Celtic

member of a culture based on a related group of languages including Gaelic, Welsh, Irish (Erse), Cornish and Breton.

centralize

to favour greater power for central rather than local government.

citizen

member of a state with full political rights (e.g. to vote) and duties (e.g. military service).

city-state

state consisting of a single major city and the surrounding area from which it drew much of its population, food supply and raw materials.

colonial rule

rule over a colony.

colony

a country ruled by a foreign state.

communism

a political movement based on the writings of Karl Marx. Marx predicted that the working classes in industrial countries would revolt to create a workers' state in which a single political party would ensure fair shares for all, and eventually government itself would not be needed. In practice, communist governments have usually been cruel dictatorships.

communist

believer in communism.

confederation

a loose grouping of states in which some may be more powerful than others.

conscription

compulsory service in the armed forces.

constitution

a written document outlining the basic laws or principles by which a country is governed.

devolution

passing some government powers of law-making and taxation to a lower-level body.

dictatorship

government by a ruler (dictator) who has more or less absolute power over the people he rules.

dual citizenship

having the rights of a citizen in two states.

duchy

territory ruled by a duke.

exile

having to live outside a person's native country.

fascism

revolutionary political movement, beginning in Italy, which promised national glory in return for total obedience to a single political party headed by an inspired leader. Fascist governments suppress free expression and free political argument.

federation

grouping of states to achieve a common benefit such as mutual defence or increased trade.

Founding Fathers

leaders of the American movement for national independence from British colonial rule.

guerrilla

a soldier who fights in small-scale hit-and-run warfare; not a member of a regular army.

idealistic

an unselfish belief in such principles as duty, justice and honour.

imperialism
the rule of foreign territories and peoples, usually for the benefit of the ruling power.

Independence Day
a national holiday celebrating when a country declared or achieved its independence; in the case of the United States, Independence Day is 4 July.

mass education
schooling for most or all of a population.

military service
serving in a country's armed forces.

Mughal
a dynasty which claimed descent from the Mongols of central Asia and ruled India from 1526 to 1857.

multinational state
state inhabited by two or more nationalities.

nationhood
the status or identity of being a nation.

nation states
states inhabited by a single nation.

native peoples
the first people to live in a country.

Orthodox
belonging to the Orthodox Church, the main form of Christianity in Greece, Serbia, Russia and neighbouring countries.

Ottoman Empire
multinational empire of south-eastern Europe and the Middle East, ruled by members of the Ottoman family until its collapse in 1920. The core area then became the Republic of Turkey.

Pan-African
having to do with the whole African continent.

Papal States
territories in central Italy ruled by the Pope.

patriotism
the love of one's own country, people and way of life.

patron saint
saint regarded as protecting or representing a particular nation.

pioneering
being the first to start something or found new settlements in an area.

plebiscite
a vote of all the people of a country for or against a single proposal.

political activists
people who are very interested and involved in politics.

post-colonial
describes a state which has become independent from being ruled as a colony.

principality
territory ruled by a prince.

quinine
medicine made from the bark of the cinchona tree and used to prevent or treat malaria.

republic
a government headed by an elected president rather than a king or emperor born to be a ruler.

republican
in the manner, mode or style of a republic.

royalist
supporter of rule by kings.

self-determination
the right of a people to govern themselves.

separatist
wanting to break away from an existing state.

socialist
someone who has the political belief in the right of government to develop greater equality between citizens.

sovereignty
supreme power, as of a state.

territory
an area of land.

Thanksgiving Day
an American annual festival commemorating the successful survival of early New England settlement. Thanksgiving Day was not adopted as a national celebration until the late nineteenth century.

Index